FIRST PEOPLES

CHEROKEE

VALERIE BODDEN

CREATIVE EDUCATION ✖ CREATIVE PAPERBACKS

Published by Creative Education and Creative Paperbacks
P.O. Box 227, Mankato, Minnesota 56002
Creative Education and Creative Paperbacks are imprints of
The Creative Company
www.thecreativecompany.us

Design and production by Christine Vanderbeek
Art direction by Rita Marshall
Printed in the United States of America

Photographs by Alamy (Everett Collection Historical,
David Lyons, National Geographic Creative, The Natural
History Museum, Niday Picture Library, North Wind
Picture Archives, Running Whirlwind), Corbis (Christie's
Images, Corbis, Danny Lehman), Getty Images (ullstein
bild), Shutterstock (Arina P Habich, jadimages, Miloje, Emre
Tarimcioglu, vectorbest)

Library of Congress Cataloging-in-Publication data
Names: Bodden, Valerie, author.
Title: Cherokee / Valerie Bodden.
Series: First Peoples.
Includes bibliographical references and index.
Summary: An introduction to the Cherokee lifestyle and
history, including their forced relocation and how they keep
traditions alive today. A Cherokee story recounts why some
creatures are able to fly.
Identifiers:
ISBN 978-1-60818-902-1 (hardcover)
ISBN 978-1-62832-518-8 (pbk)
ISBN 978-1-56660-954-8 (eBook)
This title has been submitted for CIP processing under
LCCN 2017940104.

CCSS: RI.1.1, 2, 3, 4, 5, 6, 7; RI.2.1, 2, 3, 4, 5, 6; RI.3.1, 2, 3, 5;
RF.1.1, 3, 4; RF.2.3, 4

First Edition HC   9 8 7 6 5 4 3 2 1
First Edition PBK   9 8 7 6 5 4 3 2 1

FIRST PEOPLES

TABLE *of* CONTENTS

REAL SOUTHEASTERN PEOPLE

The Cherokee lived in the American Southeast. They called themselves *Tsalagi*. This meant "Real People." "Cherokee" may be how SETTLERS pronounced the word.

 Cherokee called their homeland in the mountains the "place of blue smoke."

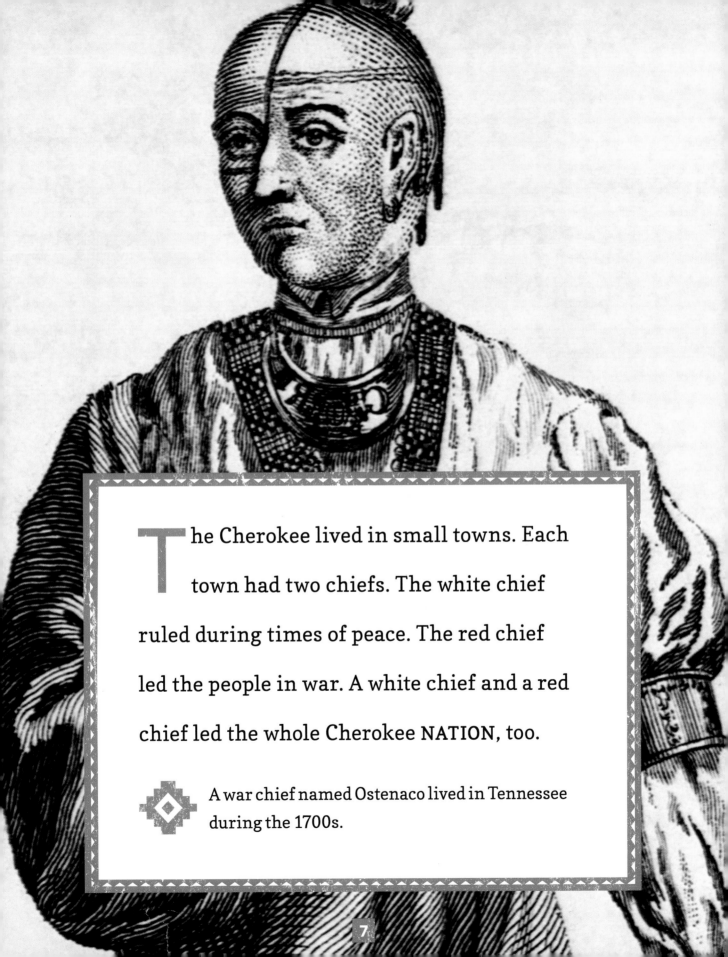

The Cherokee lived in small towns. Each town had two chiefs. The white chief ruled during times of peace. The red chief led the people in war. A white chief and a red chief led the whole Cherokee NATION, too.

A war chief named Ostenaco lived in Tennessee during the 1700s.

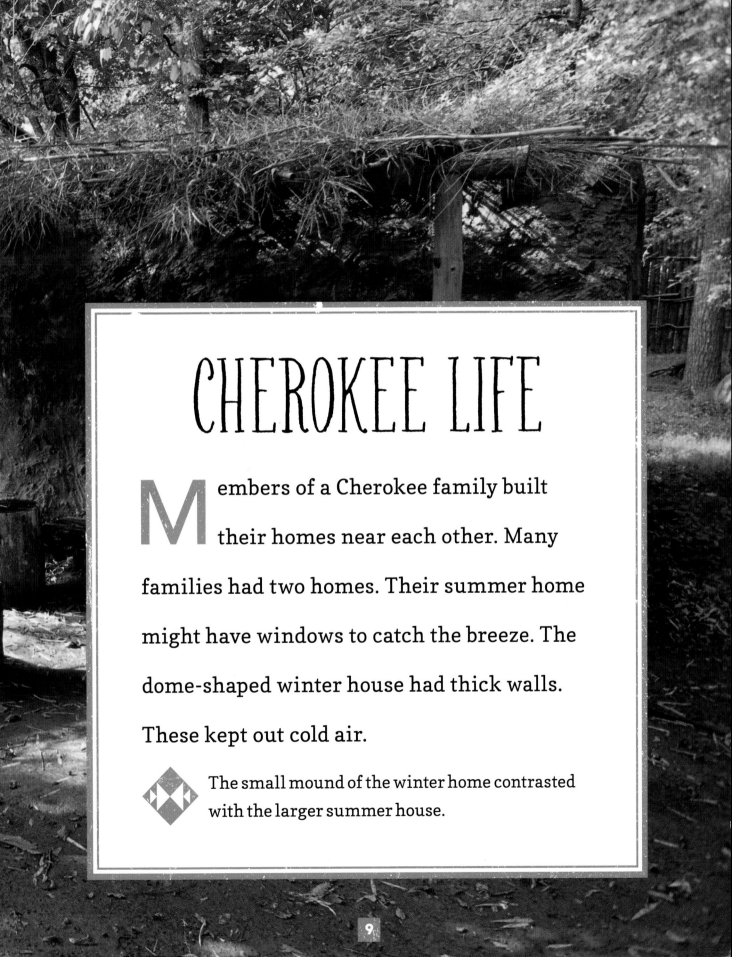

CHEROKEE LIFE

Members of a Cherokee family built their homes near each other. Many families had two homes. Their summer home might have windows to catch the breeze. The dome-shaped winter house had thick walls. These kept out cold air.

The small mound of the winter home contrasted with the larger summer house.

The Cherokee grew corn, peas, and beans. The women gathered wild plants. They made clothing. They wove baskets.

 Cherokee women still weave baskets out of river cane, white oak, and honeysuckle.

M en hunted bison, deer, and turkeys. They fought in wars. They used arrows, clubs, and axes.

Hunting with a bow and arrow made it possible to bring down larger game.

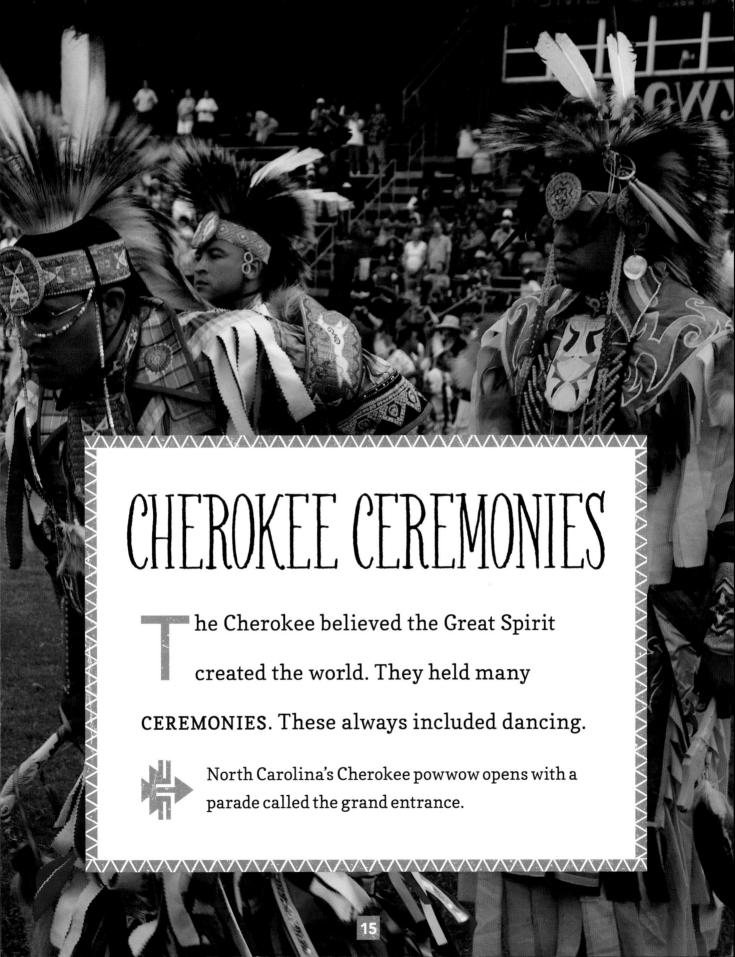

CHEROKEE CEREMONIES

The Cherokee believed the Great Spirit created the world. They held many CEREMONIES. These always included dancing.

North Carolina's Cherokee powwow opens with a parade called the grand entrance.

DISEASES AND THE TRAIL

White people settled on the Cherokees' land in the 1600s. They brought new DISEASES like smallpox. Many Cherokee people died.

Cherokee leaders met with settlers and unknowingly picked up illnesses.

In 1838, the government forced the Cherokee to leave their lands. The Cherokee had to walk to **INDIAN TERRITORY**. Many died on the way. The march became known as the Trail of Tears.

Thousands of Cherokee were rounded up by soldiers and held in forts before moving west.

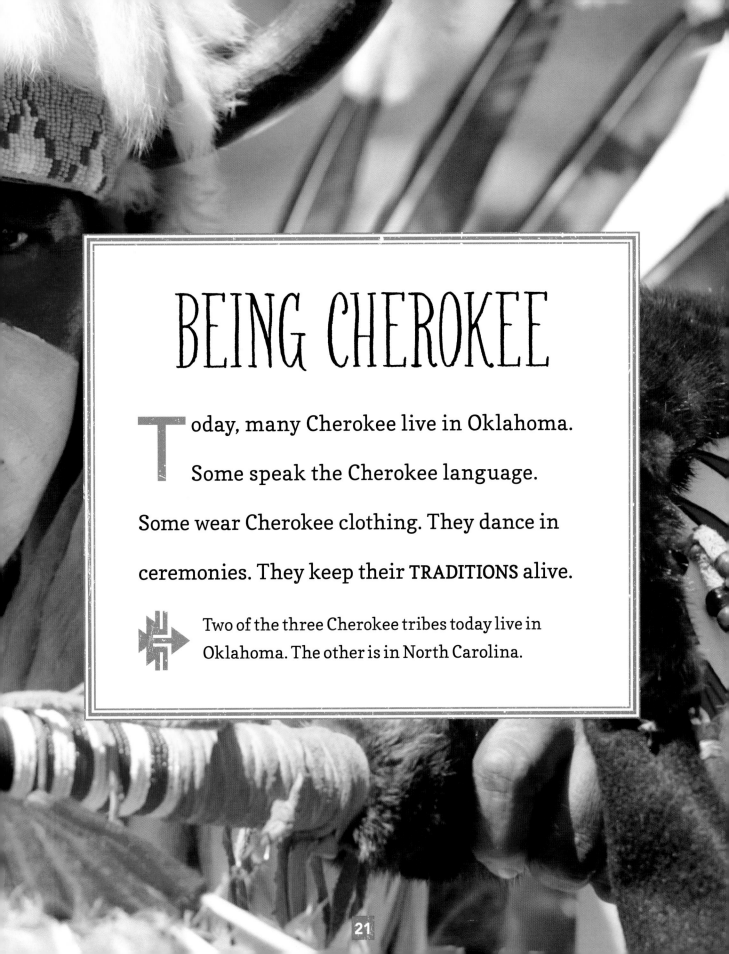

BEING CHEROKEE

Today, many Cherokee live in Oklahoma. Some speak the Cherokee language. Some wear Cherokee clothing. They dance in ceremonies. They keep their TRADITIONS alive.

Two of the three Cherokee tribes today live in Oklahoma. The other is in North Carolina.

A CHEROKEE STORY

The Cherokee told stories to explain the world around them. In one story, two little creatures wanted to play a game with the birds. But they could not fly. So Eagle asked a bird to cut wings out of leather. He put the wings on one creature. That creature became Bat. Then Eagle had two birds stretch the skin under the other creature's arms. He became Flying Squirrel. Bat and Flying Squirrel helped Eagle's team win the game!

GLOSSARY

CEREMONIES ⇥ special acts carried out according to set rules

DISEASES ⇥ sicknesses

INDIAN TERRITORY ⇥ part of the United States that was set aside for American Indians; it is now the state of Oklahoma

NATION ⇥ a specific group of American Indians, often led by its own government and sharing a common language and traditions

SETTLERS ⇥ people who come to live in a new area

TRADITIONS ⇥ beliefs, stories, or ways of doing things that are passed down from parents to their children

READ MORE

Fullman, Joe. *Native North Americans: Dress, Eat, Write, and Play Just Like the Native Americans*. Mankato, Minn.: QEB, 2010.

Morris, Ting. *Arts and Crafts of the Native Americans*. North Mankato, Minn.: Smart Apple Media, 2007.

WEBSITES

Cherokee Heritage Center: Cherokee Games
http://www.cherokeeheritage.org/cherokeeheritagecherokee_games-html/
Learn more about traditional Cherokee games.

National Park Service: Trail of Tears National Historic Park
https://www.nps.gov/media/photo/gallery.htm?id=F70DDA5A-155D-451F-67A659C12C6FC60B
Check out pictures and learn about sites along the Trail of Tears.

Note: Every effort has been made to ensure that the websites listed above are suitable for children, that they have educational value, and that they contain no inappropriate material. However, because of the nature of the Internet, it is impossible to guarantee that these sites will remain active indefinitely or that their contents will not be altered.

INDEX